Put Beginning Readers on the Right Track with
ALL ABOARD READING™

The All Aboard Reading series is especially for beginning readers. Written by noted authors and illustrated in full color, these are books that children really and truly *want* to read—books to excite their imagination, tickle their funny bone, expand their interests, and support their feelings. With five different reading levels, All Aboard Reading lets you choose which books are most appropriate for your children and their growing abilities.

Picture Readers—for Ages 3 to 6
Picture Readers have super-simple texts, with many nouns appearing as rebus pictures. At the end of each book are 24 flash cards—on one side is the rebus picture; on the other side is the written-out word.

Pre-Level 1—for Ages 4 to 6
First Friends, First Readers have a super-simple text starring lovable recurring characters. Each book features two easy stories that will hold the attention of even the youngest reader while promoting an early sense of accomplishment.

Level 1—for Preschool through First-Grade Children
Level 1 books have very few lines per page, very large type, easy words, lots of repetition, and pictures with visual "cues" to help children figure out the words on the page.

Level 2—for First-Grade to Third-Grade Children
Level 2 books are printed in slightly smaller type than Level 1 books. The stories are more complex, but there is still lots of repetition in the text, and many pictures. The sentences are quite simple and are broken up into short lines to make reading easier.

Level 3—for Second-Grade through Third-Grade Children
Level 3 books have considerably longer texts, harder words, and more complicated sentences.

All Aboard for happy reading!

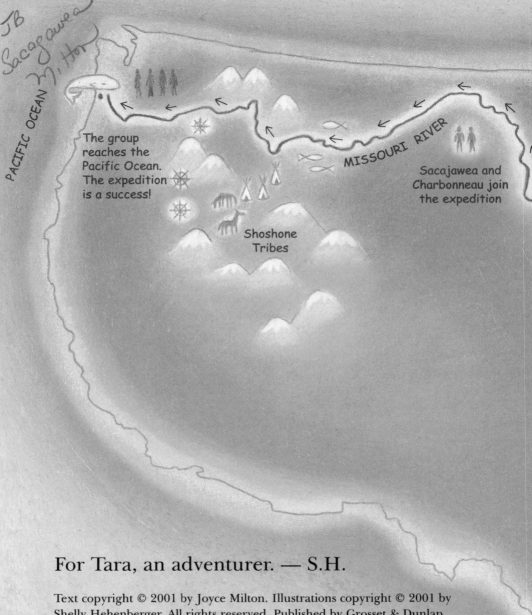

For Tara, an adventurer. — S.H.

Text copyright © 2001 by Joyce Milton. Illustrations copyright © 2001 by
Shelly Hehenberger. All rights reserved. Published by Grosset & Dunlap,
a division of Penguin Putnam Books for Young Readers, New York.
GROSSET & DUNLAP and ALL ABOARD READING are trademarks of
Penguin Putnam Inc. Published simultaneously in Canada. Printed in the U.S.A.

Library of Congress Cataloging-in-Publication Data is available

ISBN 0-448-42616-1 (GB) A B C D E F G H I J
ISBN 0-448-42539-4 (pbk) A B C D E F G H I J

ALL
ABOARD
READING™
Level 2
Grades 1-3

SACAJAWEA

HER TRUE STORY

The Lewis and Clark
expedition begins in
St. Louis, Missouri.

BY JOYCE MILTON
ILLUSTRATED BY SHELLY HEHENBERGER

Grosset & Dunlap • New York

This is the true story

of a young American Indian girl.

She lived 200 years ago.

Her name was Sacajawea.

(You say it like this—

Sah kah juh WEE ah.)

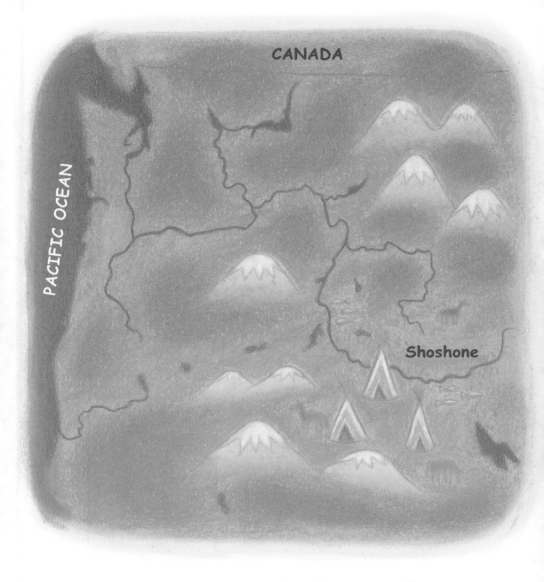

Sacajawea was a Shoshone Indian
(Show SHOW nee).
The Shoshones lived
in the northwest.

The Shoshones loved horses.

They used bows

and arrows to hunt.

Other tribes had guns.

From time to time,
other Indians came
and stole their horses.

One day, Sacajawea

was picking berries.

Suddenly she heard gunfire.

It was a raid!

Sacajawea took off across the river.

But she did not get far.

A warrior grabbed her

and carried her off.

Sacajawea grew up as a captive

of the enemy chief.

A fur trader came into camp one day.

His name was Charbonneau

(Shar bon OH).

He and the chief gambled.

When the game was over,

the trader had won Sacajawea.

She was still a teenager.

But now she was the trader's wife.

The trader and his young wife
made their way to North Dakota.
One day, American explorers
appeared on the river.
They came in a big barge
and two small boats.
The Americans had even brought along
their pet dog, Seaman.
Curious Indians lined the banks to watch.

President Thomas Jefferson had asked
the explorers to find a route
from the Missouri River
to the Pacific Ocean.
Their group was led by two men.
One was named Meriwether Lewis.
The other was Captain William Clark.
The Indians called Clark
"the red-headed chief."

MERIWETHER LEWIS

WILLIAM CLARK

Sacajawea's husband
knew how to talk to the Indians
in words and sign language.
Lewis and Clark asked him
to join their group.

Ice was forming on the river.
The explorers built a log fort
and waited for the spring.
In the evenings, one of the men
would play his violin.

The others would dance.

Sacajawea just sat and watched.

The white man's music

sounded strange to her.

She didn't feel like dancing anyway.

She was going to have a baby very soon.

One day in February,

Sacajawea felt the baby coming.

The pain went on for many hours.

Finally, Lewis gave her some medicine.

He made it himself,

from the tail of a dead rattlesnake.

Ten minutes later,

Sacajawea had a son.

She called him Pomp.

By April, the ice had melted.

The explorers were ready to set out

with their boats and canoes.

The Indians had told Lewis and Clark

that mountains lay ahead of them.

To get across,

they would need horses—

Shoshone horses.

Only Sacajawea spoke Shoshone.

So she went along with the explorers,

with little Pomp on her back.

Right from the start,

Sacajawea showed her courage.

One time, a gust of wind

tipped her boat.

Charbonneau panicked.

He dropped the rudder.

Boxes of supplies slid

into the water.

Sacajawea leaned over the side
and grabbed the boxes
before they were swept away.
Without her quick thinking,
the explorers would have been
in big trouble!

Soon the group came to a stretch

of rapids and waterfalls.

To go any farther,

they would have to load their boats

onto wooden sleds

and drag them around the falls.

The job took many weeks.

Captain Clark and Charbonneau
went on ahead to scout the route.
They took Sacajawea with them.
Even with Pomp on her back,
she could walk as fast as the men.

One morning,

they were exploring

a deep ravine.

It started to rain.

So everyone huddled

under a rock ledge.

Suddenly, Sacajawea heard

a loud roar.

A wall of water and mud

was bearing down on them.

It was a flash flood!

Everyone scrambled for high ground.

Sacajawea had Pomp in her arms.

She couldn't climb very fast.

Charbonneau pulled her after him.

Captain Clark pushed from behind.

They got out of the ravine

just in time.

The explorers pushed on.

The wide river was now

a small stream.

One day, Sacajawea saw a tall rock.

She knew this place!

The Shoshones called it

"Beaver's Head."

Their summer hunting grounds

must be nearby.

Lewis and a few scouts went ahead.

Soon they met three Shoshone women.

The women were scared.

Were the strangers going to hurt them?

But Lewis put red paint on their cheeks.

This was a sign of peace.

How did he know that?

Sacajawea had told him.

The Shoshone chief and
some of the Indians
went to the explorers' camp.
The chief met with
Lewis and Clark
inside a big tent.

When Sacajawea went inside the tent,
her heart filled with joy.
The chief was her brother!
She burst into tears
and rushed to his side.

The chief agreed to sell them horses.

Now the explorers could

get across the great

Rocky Mountains.

It was only September,

but the mountain trails were icy.

The horses carried the supplies.

The men had to walk.

Their feet grew numb from the cold.

For once, Sacajawea

had an easier time.

She and Pomp got to ride.

There wasn't much food left.

Sacajawea dug up some roots

that were good to eat.

But it was not enough

for the hungry men.

Day after day, the men went hunting

and returned empty-handed.

Once, they were so hungry

that they killed a horse

and cooked it.

Sacajawea was hungry, too.

But she would not eat horse meat.

At last, the highest mountains
were behind them.
The explorers had reached
the lands of a tribe called
the Nez Perce (Nezz-Purse).
They wore fancy robes with shells
and porcupine quills.

On this side of the mountains
the rivers ran west
toward the Pacific Ocean.
The explorers set to work
building canoes.
The Nez Perce agreed to take care
of the group's horses.

But now they faced new dangers.

The river was swift

and full of rapids.

One canoe hit a rock

and flipped over.

Luckily, no one drowned.

Along the banks of the river,
there were many Indian villages.
At first, the Indians were ready
to attack the strangers.
But when they saw
Sacajawea and little Pomp,
they changed their minds.
No war party would bring
a mother and baby along.

About 20 miles from the ocean,

the explorers made camp

for the winter.

One day there was news.

A monster had washed up

on the beach!

Captain Clark knew that

the monster must be a whale.

He decided to take a few men

and get some of the whale meat.

Sacajawea begged to go along.

She had come all this way.

She wanted to see the great sea.

Clark agreed.

On a cold day in January in 1806,

Sacajawea got her wish.

She looked out over the Pacific Ocean.

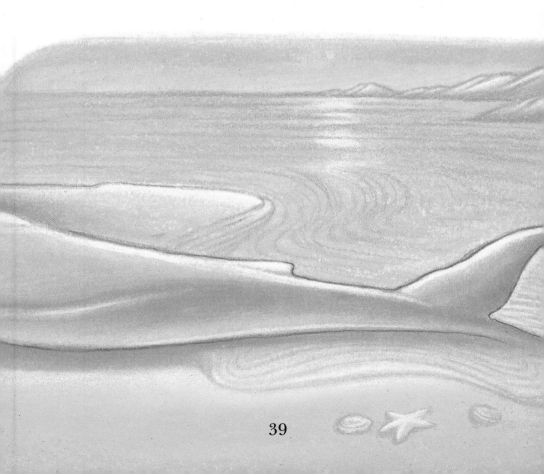

When spring came,

the explorers were ready

for their return trip.

PACIFIC OCEAN

Sacajawea's journey home
from the Pacific Ocean.

On the way back,

they faced more hardships.

But Sacajawea was always cheerful.

Captain Clark admired her for that.

He gave her the nickname "Janey."

He called Pomp "my dancing boy."

At one point,

Pomp came down with a high fever.

Clark tried everything to save him.

He even made a cream out of bear fat

to rub on the little boy's neck.

It worked!

Soon Pomp was well again.

At last, the explorers reached
their old winter fort in North Dakota.
They had been away for
one year and four months.
The Indians welcomed them
with loud cheers and gifts of corn.

Now it was time for Sacajawea

to say good-bye to Lewis and Clark.

Captain Clark offered to adopt Pomp

and send him to school.

Sacajawea said no.

Pomp was too young to leave her.

Two years later, Charbonneau
and his family moved to St. Louis.
They bought a little farm
from Captain Clark.

But the fur trader couldn't get used

to the quiet life of a farmer.

He and his wife joined

a group of traders

headed for the Dakotas.

In the winter of 1812,
news came that Charbonneau's
young wife had died there
of a bad fever.

Was this the end of Sacajawea?
Maybe not.
The Shoshones say that
the woman who died
was another wife of Charbonneau.
They say Sacajawea had left
her husband and had gone to live
with the Comanche tribe.

Many years later, an old woman
returned to the lands of the Shoshones.
She talked about Lewis and Clark's
journey to the Pacific.
She showed people a medal
with President Jefferson's picture on it.
Was this woman the real Sacajawea?
If so, she lived to be almost 100 years old.

There are still many mysteries

about the life of Sacajawea.

But we do know that

she was strong and full of courage.

She was part of a great adventure.

Today we honor her

with a golden dollar coin.